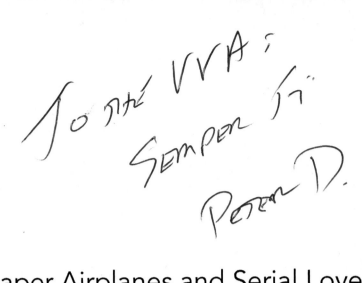

To the VVA;
Semper Fi
Peter D.

Paper Airplanes and Serial Lovers
The Making of a Poet

p. a. delorenzi

outskirts press
DENVER, COLORADO

CONTENTS

WHY PAPER AIRPLANES?

I owed my first recollection of a lengthy conversation with my father to mathematics. Knowing his true proficiency at the business I approached him for an explanation to a simple procedure called long division. That was my introduction to that singular point beyond the Universe that we call "Infinity". It was not until much later in my life that I realized how simply my father had explained the answer. I was seven years old. My father had just been teaching me the first rudiments of analytical calculus. He had previously taught me different wing designs for paper airplanes when I was four. I still remember experimenting with different aileron configurations in order to turn corners and ambush my sister or mom. Since that time I have flown paper airplanes from the Empire State Building when I was about 10; the top of a forward combat air traffic control tower when I was 19 years old serving in Vietnam; the Washington Monument when I turned 21; and from the third tier in C-Block at the incarcerated age of thirty. I was also piloting the sleek paper craft while sitting in my father's favorite chair waiting for my sister to phone upon her arrival back in Buffalo the day after he died. It was the day after Veteran's Day, 1983. In my mind I was still in the war, but in reality I had just been released from prison.

THE WAR YEARS

Two of my four sons were born during these years. Neither have I met. The first was born in 1967. That was just shortly after I entered the Marine Corps. His mom promised to hunt me down and love me forever when I returned from the war. I never heard from her again nor knew the boys name. The relocation was her mom's idea.

Another son was born in 1969 while I was in Vietnam.
I never heard anything about him until several years after returning home from the war. I ran into a mutual friend in 1972 that showed me photos and gave a good report on the lad. I never have met him. That was my second son. I do not know his name either.

Upon my return from Vietnam in 1969 I was anxious to visit my Grandfather in Niagara Falls, where I had spent a lot of time as a youth. Niagara Falls was dry. That was the second time in my short life that I had seen the Falls dry. Once due to Mother Nature and a deep freeze, and once due to the Corps of Engineers trying to understand Mother Nature. So now comes this year, 2016, when I have finally watched the Cubs win the World Series. Miracles can happen and curses can be broken.

"Yours till Niagara Falls runs dry" did not mean the same as it used to before the war.

Quang Tri 1968

WAR NEVER ENDS..... 1980

war never ends
it seeks to destroy
and in its' cancerous
ways kills silently
better than any commando
and more sadistically
slowly, all the while
dredging from murky minds
memories of war
wars that sadistically kill
its' most valiant
its' most pure warriors
who fight on bravely
but war never ends

Vandegrift Combat Base during Operation Dewey Canyon

MY DREAM.... 1981

dark skies
explode with light
exposing evil shapes
a hundred men on wire
twisting in torture
then cut apart
by the fast lights
bursting the silence
and again the darkness
which makes us tired

LLOH 6

I was 19 years old and fighting a war. Already in my young life I had been electrocuted, drowned, in a serious 100 mph wreck, a half dozen good fights and in love twice. But I had never seen a dead man except in a casket at a funeral home. Things changed in a hurry when our convoy came across this grisly scene where villagers were stoning a VC to death outside their village gates. I had been in country less than 36 hours. Welcome to the Nam.

We drove on to LZ Stud (later renamed Vandegrift Combat Base) where I would spend most of the next 8 months of my life at the entrance to the Ashau Valley. The DMZ was just a couple of miles away as was the Laotian border and Ho Chi Minh Trail. It was an intense time. My unit considered it a 30 day detail, but I never requested relief, opting to stay where the action was. I was at war.

Air control tower at VCB

PAST TONIGHT..... 1980

Is past dead?
no, nor never will be,
as long as the scream
of some stuck Lance
is alive in my
dreams tonite

Our Hill sign

Door gunners view

MED EVAC HEROES

I was your eyes when
you could not see
your ears when
you were deaf
the salesman
that said
yes you can
and you did
most of the time
most of the days

bringing us back
our own brothers
from places unknown
and not knowing
to places cold in granite
surrounded in lawn
kept carefully short
and proper
like our rifles
disassembled
for inspection

hoping for hope
that we did okay
wanting to do okay
to do better
for them
the dead
we knew before
when life
smiled back at us
forever
and glad

Homeless vets

CONVERSATION WITH A WEST BURNSIDE VETERAN..... 1980

Whiskers, wine breath and rags
"Vietnam did this" you say
"you did this to yourself" I say
"A prisoner of war" you say,
"three years and some"
"Bullshit" says I
"only death in war."

once a prisoner, you are
now bound to beg
for wine and food
arm around my shoulder
holding yourself captive,
ten years since chains
"Can war last this long?"

"I was there too, my friend,
Khe Sanh, Dong Ha,
Hue City in its' heyday
shot at, shooting back,
rockets and fire
filling sandbags
with our own feces

I remember a time
when even our own Army,
confused, shelled us,
sorry bout that
cave dwellers we were,
buried in mud
to stay out of the rain,
damn rain
much like yourself, now,
hunkering down in doorways
to sleep with your pity
begging money and food
much like the wretched
gook children in the Nam
who also had no one to care
and ran in packs
like hungry coyotes

is it regret you feel?
though you were there,
fighting for your life,
it was not your war
just a job as I saw it,
that had to be done,
and some had to do it

and some had to die for it,
either fast and easy
or slow and hard,
like you, and others
sad but true fact that
the spoils of war
are rotting flesh.
and reality lies
in a rotting mind
and you, my friend,
are rotting away;
it is seen in your face
as you drink your wine
and heard in your voice
as you beg for food.

Children looking for anything

THE LATTERS OF LIFE.....

There was a time
when we were previous
previously young,
healthy and loving
now comes the time
when we now shun the latters
that we strived to climb,
to balance on that last step,
perched as a bird

toes wrapped tightly
upon that wrung
our songs that thru the years
had been sung
seem all to be of you,
your escapades, your lives
your wrongs and rights,
your loves and hates,
and especially the forgiveness

that comes as the feathers
gray and white
scrag from the chin
to only hide
the previous
and identify the latters
no matter how many
wrongs have been wrought
no matter how many
battles have been fought

the warrior still shines
through the fog
but stands alone,
afraid to advance
yet yearning for
the latter's previously raised
when the lofty goals
were met with ease
and the loves,
ah yes the loves,
ah sweet, sweet loves

Arlington National Cemetery

ODE TO THE VA....1972

Stretcher Bearer, Stretcher Bearer
pick the pieces of my heart
and place them in your basket

they do not hear
they do not love
they do not feel no more
the slickness of blood
the yawnings of wounds
caused by your damned war

Stretcher Bearer, Stretcher Bearer
pick the pieces of my heart
and place them in your basket
they cry, they writhe, in agony
O can't you see, O can't you see
what the war has done to me?

Stretcher Bearer, Stretcher Bearer
forget the pieces of my heart
just give to me my casket

The Momuments of Washington...

Please don't let this happen again...

Photo taken prior to the dedication of the Vietnam Veterans Memorial Nov 11, 1982
...photo by peter delorenzi

Vietnam Veterans Memorial Dedication 1982

Never Ending
WANDERINGS & LUSTS
(a life gone awry & back again)

Two more sons were born during these times. Finally, I have met one of my sons, Joseph, but have lost oh so much to my life. One of my steadfast friends shared many a poetic moment with me through these years until her passing. From California to Louisiana, Colorado, Montana and Oregon the old Harley was my constant companion and was party to many a memorable moment.

"Lulubelle" 1951 Harley

A North Mountain Climb..... 1972

I wonder
if I loosen the rock at the
bottom of this mountain
if the whole mountain
will fall
or maybe it is the rock
at the top?

North Cascades

TIME..... 1972

Out of the sea
walked the Lizard
testing his new legs
while turning his tail
upon the water
from which he spawned
o'er so many
millions of years
he roamed the Earth
a minute observer
of the changes
wrought by time
yet he spoke
not a word of protest
simultaneously the Sea
testing its' new legs
crept unto the land
crunching, grating
killing, freezing
ever Southward it came
unto the Lizard's home, and,
as if it had looked upon
Gomorrah
the Lizard was petrified,
his one last slither, step
and swing of his tail preserved
next to him in the mud that
time turned to Stone
many unseen eons passed
the Lizard's eyes
but, alas, many eons

is not forever
for that trait belongs
only to Time,
for Time alone
is never ending
and nothing survives Time.
not the rocks, nor trees
not the water in the oceans
nor even the air that we breathe,
not the Lover's Love
nor the Devil's Hate,
nay, not even the Earth herself
will survive the calamities of Time
and Man, you wonder?
ha, his time on Earth
is so short till dust,
that even the infernal Father
will have blinked
barely once,
leaving the only thing left
In the void
that once was the Universe
to be Time

Ancient cliff paintings Lake Superior

FATHERLESS PUPS 1973

The bitch stopped
when I whistled,
hungry looking eyes,
belly swollen
with unborn young
soon to be brought forth
born near the yards of
steel and tracks,
of bells and whistles;
the home of the mother
with no father
to raise her
fatherless young.

most will be stolen
by the railway workers
and go to good homes,
always warm,
always loving and fed,
they will learn
to sit and speak
but of the Mother
will they remember
the mangy coat,
the hungry eyes;
and she,
will she remember
their father?

Nonno Mio..... 1975

each day our train
passes by him,
standing motionless
apart from the crowd,
alone

he glares at me
standing on
the locomotive step,
large eyes
entrancing, embracing
a lonely bull looking
as Nonno Mio

watching as
before, in youth,
a child looking up,
age looking down,
from fiery Italian eyes
foreboding, forceful
yet kind.

OLD BONES AND NEW FRIENDS.....2011

Nice vertebrae!
Just look at that Lumbar!
could that be you? Wow!
recycled and ready
to be reloved
after parting
with such tragedy
the smoothness
of your cervicals
cradled in my hands
as we find each
other's bones cradled
by a new friend

Falling.... 2011

Further and deeper
to heights unkown
in lives before us
until tonight's lite
lites our path

our hands hold tight
our souls have sight
our minds have might
our hearts have right

and we start anew
having taken our cue
chalked for the run
of the last table
to pocket love together

HANDS AND HEARTS..... 2016

if i cannot hold your hand
i cannot feel your heart beat
nor listen to your soul
as it speaks to mine
without sharing
sleep with you
i am sleepless
in my dreams
and alone
in my nightmares
watching from afar

now as your hair turns to gray
and your child grows older
your life blossoms anew
while mine fades away
incomplete
all because
i cannot hold your hand

THE SCOPE OF NATURE.....2016

I tire of the promulgation of hatred
violence and selfish interests
yearning for the promulgation of love
the freedoms that are our gifts
the opportunities that have expanded
in both scope and nature

to explode in a new universe
where sharing, hope and peace
are the norms and the loves
yes, the loves that are gifts
which makes opportunity possible
in both nature and scope

Skylites...... 2011

I still sleep beneath the stars
as if the cave had never left me
alone without lighted sky
to dance with the Great Bears
to dodge the moon's antics above
while wandering below it all
amongst lunatical splendors
of love

Elegy for a dog friend..........1978

Ol Scratch lay dying,
bleeding to death,
His only reward for his trespass,
Midst a pool of blood
on woodshed floor
His heart barely pumping,
then pumping no more
In trouble no more,
no more devil's heart,
Scartch let out one last fart

SOUTH TO NORTH..... 2013

Coming home
the bumps of atmosphere
like life itself reminds us
of the lofty heights
where we pray and dream
among the clouds
whether sun of moon
calm or turbulent
wet or dry
as the canyons formed
on our cheeks
by our tears of sorrow and joy
through the ages
fast forward
as the speed of the wings
lifts and carries your soul
back into the world
of east and west where
it is still east and west
and love awaits
and remains for the taking
at your leisure
and pleasure......forever

To a Friend..... 2012

Our lives were typed
and drawn to end
though distant
your constant closeness
gives warmth and hope
a thread of reality
to an unreal past
a friend here
a fantasy there
but always an artist
and loved

DREAM OF MY LIFE....

You are the love
dream of my life
that I will never have
nor ever lost
in my life of loves
as you are
the dream of my life
that I may never have
but will always love.

Heading west 1977

FEB 15, 2011

So if I write something to you
that really, really unravels your knots,
would you hesitate to open my door
in the midst of the night?
I would hope
that you would find my warmth
enough to comfort you through the cold;
and allow you to wake in the morn
with the briskness, freshness and brightness
each day that follows
each loving night
My Friend is my Lover
My Lover is my Friend

On Watch 2012

I know you are out there
standing above the seas,
watching the stars
as they have been for millennia
your hair blowing softly,
first to the east,
then suddenly to the west
as you throw a smile
to the waters below
you are happy
I know you are out there.

The lightning strikes
far off in the distance
ominous rolling thunder follows
the wind shifts and your smile turns
to one of playful ambitions
clouds cover the stars quickly,
and no longer do the they reflect
upon the crests of each wave
as there is no more light
but I know you are out there

MONEY MANAGEMENT..... 1983

A bad manager of money I am
but then, so is my uncle,
my great Uncle Sam
for we both are broke
which goes in accord
with each other's policies
to send our money overseas

so we borrow and beg,
but steal we wont
and hope that the people will care,
but care much they don't;

over charge and double charge
over talk and doubletalk
I think I'll take
a nice long walk, and
think of how bad
a manager of money I am,
and I'll think of my uncle,
my great Uncle Sam

Selected Works
of
Linda Strasser

Every poet needs an idol, a friend that will read, with an ear for your thoughts and understanding in their heart.

As shared with p.a. delorenzi

MATURITY

Linda Strasser..... 1973

The time I had set aside in my head
Wont come.
I see that now.

A desolation fills me;
All illusions gone.

The great orange dreams
I leave to children.
It is the only way we get here-
To clutch balloons of hope on twine-

And then they pop and leave us
Holding dangling strings;
But seeing finally where we are-
The view unblocked, clear-cut and true.

It is not maturity,
It is resignation.

(NO TITLE)

Linda Strasser..... 1973

I scream, my mouth un open
I weep, but have no tears;
Within me are volcanoes
But my face shows only years.

When I have peeled the last potato,
Set the meat upon the rack,
Washed the lettace, set the table,
Felt the stab in lower back.

Then I know my nightly madness,
Dreams of glory, love and hell,
Is my one sole source of gladness,
And at that I'm doing well.

For my head is never quiet
And my body never still;
Take this housewifery and motherhood,
As for me, I've had my fill!

TRIAD

Linda Strasser..... 1973

Three natures sever me
Divide my head
Claim dominion ever soul and body

I am of the sea
Rip tides, kelp, salt taste
All me

A songbird high astride the air
Riding waves of wind
Intent on minute specks and sun
All fair

And yet in troubled times
I long for earth's sweet smell-
To ring about with weed and flower,
Rose and briar

Have mercy on a creature divided in three ways
Feet of fish
Brain of bird
Soul of hare.

Monday

Linda Strasser..... 1973

Why do I hide in the marvelous polish
That makes the marble shine?
Why do I duck behind the broom
That sweeps the stoop so fine?
Why do I wrap myself in piles
Of laundry-colored and white?
Why do I watch the daytime shows
And never join the fight?
Why do I wash
And why do I scrub,
And why do I toe the line?
I'll tell you why;
Because if I didn't we'de all be
Up to our necks in shit.

DREAM

Linda Strasser..... 1973

What time is this apart
Astride a hearse with syncopated gait
Each hood beat on the sand
Repeats our yesterday, tomorrows,
News so short, so all consuming..
The earth upon a turtles back,
Almost still with us and time...
Beneath benign, beleaguered moon,
Ever fresh with mint upon our lips,
Awash with cream and music.
Dreams awakened to, and real-
Felt more with nerve ends;
Teeth and nails.
Have I not said a thousand times
And yet again-
To hold you in my mind-
My animals, your aims, alive by day
As well as night.
(Distance: place but not soul)
Converges in some middle air and strides on.

(UNTITLED)

Linda Strasser..... 1973

Speak to me mother.
Sooth my sorrows with your words
Make sounds that comfort me and hold me.
Tell me wondrous things
And true, please make them true.

Oh I am weary of this time,
These battles that are ever near,
These horrors that are garish bright.

Speak to me in muted colors.
Sand and still water, pale skies.
Bathe me in softest light and cool shade.
And calm, I need the calm.

Oh I am tired of this place, these frantic scrambles for success,
These faces that are twisted masks.

Speak from your eyes in silken threads
That wrap me up cocoon-like
So I may stop this jerking and lie still.

Weave me a blanket with your tongue
And cover me with vowels
O and O and O and O.

You do not have to touch me,
Only speak.

THE LISTENER

Linda Strasser..... 1973

I've seen the tumbling waters bail
Beneath the aged sky
I've held this trembling day before
And knew that it must die.

I've pressed my face to forest floors
And heard the awful cry
Of races come and gone again
Before the world could sigh

I've eaten grapes which came from vines
That lived a thousand years
I've watched the cycles of the moon
And tasted salt in tears

But never have I wished to leave
This world and life behind
Until I heard you say to them
You stayed just to be kind

EARTH

Linda Strasser..... 1973

This earth has held me,
Drawn me nearer still
In times of pain and fear
To rest abut with hands and knees,
To pluck the weeds
Sweet resting in my nostrils,
To quell the trembling
Of my limbs in earth
Once black, then red and cracked,
But earth the same.
Does this peace come
From digging my own grave,
Each tender plant an offshoot
Of myself,
Alive and well,
Living somewhere underground?

THE HERMIT

Linda Strasser..... 1973

In silence, sitting on the wall
I changed to see a tulip fall
And land with such a thunderous crash,
(I picked it up, but it was ash.)

While swinging gently on the swing,
I smiled to hear a robin sing
Whose song then broadened to a shriek,
(It's final feather brushed my cheek.)

I strolled to town to see the sights,
The populace broke out in fights,
With stomping, pounding, jeering fits,
(The place, I hear is now in bits.)

So I've retreated-just as well;
The world is really going to hell.

CIRCLE

Linda Strasser..... 1973

This ever present me
Presents a problem to my sphere:
All round by definition
But with edges sharp and clear defined
That cut and bruise.
One life to live a thousand way.
So many corners not gone into yet.
Ricochet around my walls
So slick, so smooth
Then jagged, cragged.
Where do I reside?
By day, for some, in sunlit windows
Free from specks of dust;
By night, in caves laced with beloved mold
And firelight,
Teeth shining, hair undone.
Who wanders into my circle deserves his fate.

HENRY HOWARD CASSELMAN

Linda Strasser..... 1973

Henry Howard Casselman was a bad, bad, man.
He had five children
And one of them had me.
He taught his children very well
The rules one needs to live.
One-always respect your elders.
Two- always respect your betters
And ignore everyone else was three.
He taught them wisely for his time
And past conditioning.
So what did he produce?
One drunk
One slug
Two dead women
And a third who somewhere found the strength
Not to be drowned.
And what did they produce?
The men-not one.
The women-four among them:
Four troubled, double-edged, chain-breaking,
Ground shaking monsters
Bent on self-construction, self-destruction,
Self-absorption, self-denial, selfish selflessness-
Just like all the rest.

CANDIDATE'S WIFE

Linda Strasser..... 1973

Weighted, coiled, stuffed and coifed,
I stand beside you in receiving lines.
The question seems to be
How will I be received?
The arched and penciled brows lift
Tees point north-then north-east and west.
Do you detect a hint of disfavor?

Have I closed an eye,
Stifled a yawn,
Made a scene by playing staccato tunes with my tongue?
For shame?
They see
They mark an X next to my name
And your's especially.
I am an appendage,
Some days an asset,
But when I have been the ultimate me,
(Too much for anyone to bear, you say)
A liability.
All those dinners-
Yards and yards of linen like a shrewd
Washed and ironed cash time
Between the salad and the schops-
Drinks in the Drawing room,
Coffee in the library,

Tours with paintings done by me.

Linda Strasser..... 1973

"Entertain,
But do not dance, my dear, past ten
And know the liquor that you hold, holds you."
(And hinted at in sly unetuous tones to relatives and friends).
Will get me yet
In settlement or time of fire.
A finger pointed
"See?
It is as I've said
She drinks."
Insinuation-
Scorn
I used to fear...
No more

CENTER-FOLD

Linda Strasser..... 1973

Your alabaster women,
Silken soft and fine,
Are not at all like me:
Instead of marble,
Pink and smooth and clear,
I give you such topography
As war zones are made of–
Jungle, brush and cactus,
Mountain, marsh–
A trip ever my landscape with fingertips
Could never be dull–
Something new everywhere–
So explore, explore
And give up your satiny women–
They bore, they bore!

MIDDLE YEARS

Linda Strasser..... 1973

I weep for us-
Brave daughters of our mothers
Going forth to do battle
Without hats and gloves.
Instructed in the important things;
The foxtrot, French and petit point-
R.S.V.P
We are still girls
Regardless of our years.
Great hulking girls,
Filled with guilt because we
Do not sit like ladies,
Look like ladies,
Act like ladies.
We do not believe such shit.
I weep for us-
Brave mothers of our daughters
Who go forth to find justice
With their pens and tongues.
Admonished new and again
About the important things:
Truth, peace and sisterhood.
I held my mother's hand,
My child's
And try to bridge the gap.
Mine are the middle years.

RELUCTANCE

Linda Strasser….. 1973

Reluctant, I go among men
Tired to my bones with eyes
That look away,
Hands that do not touch,
Lips that do not speak a word.
I want to hear a voice-not there;
To touch a hand-too far;
To meet an eye-somewhere.

Hesitant, I lie down on my bed,
Afraid to sleep because in dreams
I touch eyes-
Hear hands-
And look words to one who does not care.

UNDOING

Linda Strasser..... 1973

A desolate time to ask such moral questions
I have only myself to blame
For these banners signs and flags
That speak their lie and catch me up.
My cross
I'm cross,
Don't cross-
Rabid words writ loud on every corner
Running sharks teeth through my mind
Forming patterns in the darkness
Taking turns to do their thing
Pressing ever in upon me
Marching forward with the banner
Struggling hapless with the cause
Resting hopeful only after
Can't you read the words?
"Why have I been undone?"

Linda passed about 10 years later from cancer. She is still missed
each day.

The Prison Years

1980 found me on trial for my life for the killing of a man in Oregon that was assaulting a woman. It's a long story. A very good friend was my pillar of support through the ordeal. While I was in Lane County Jail enjoying solitary confinement before my trial, Mt. St. Helen's erupted, as well as riots in Florida. That was the beginning of the Weaklies, which comprise Part Two of this work. The friend still dials me now and then, usually when the weather is nasty outside and she is drinking.

Eventually convicted of Manslaughter I was transferred to the Oregon State Penitentiary. While in prison I met an old friend, Easy, another Harley rider I had known in SoCal. Now he was balding and barely distinguishable. He taught me the ropes of life in the big house. Most of his life he had been locked up. My dad sent the NY Times Sunday edition.

There are not many events that I care to share about prison life. It is a tough way to wake up each morning. Stay free.

A Prisoner's Knowledge..... 1980

I know now how the Leopard feels
haunches rippling
the well conditioned muscles
of captivity pacing endlessly
across his twelve foot cage
head held low
sometimes a soft growl
eyes glowering
at those watching him
looking forward only to dinner
and the peace of solitude
yet somewhere in his glazed eyes
he runs wild again
through the tall grasses
of a far away land

FORGET ME CANT'S..... 1980

Peace on earth, what a shallow plea
amidst a life of hostility
for the younger souls know
only of war
from near to far they practice what
we, the old warriors know
and wish to forget
forget me can't
the flowers we have sown
and cut to vase to call our own
for in our windows
we will display our blooms
and hope the youngers
will see their dooms
to grow old quickly
and wish to forget

Easy 1980

Yo Easy, yer right
those missing years of youth
should've been filled
with baseball games
and climbing trees
to watch a caterpillar
lunch on leaves
the innocent first love
followed by the inevitable
lusts of youth

instead of the stripped cells
and concrete floors
of a cold reformatory
in a state of non-reform
conform, conform
to the wicked norm
so that now years later
in still another institution
we tie and untie bed sheets
wondering whether
it'd be best to hang out
or just cry, man.

PIGEONS 1981

motionless
the pigeons atop the roof
stab infrequently
the unseen lice
which disturbs
their meditation
while grey feathers ruffle
and soothe to a
wordless song
the melody of constant hope
to be free from irritation

Population 1980

marshes, bayous, mires
of mud and quicksand
filled with devious,
treacherous and hissing
creatures
who love the muck
and rape the earths' virginity

while walking
through this quagmire
speak not of the Lord
and they shall
let you pass.......

Sleepwalk....1980

the bare concrete floor
meets my naked feet
time after silent time
as I traverse
my steel enclosure
and let my mind rappel down
the glass smooth face
of the distant cliffs
of freedom

SOUNDS WITHOUT SIGHTS 1981

Parker and John are trying to sing soul
while Crazy Louie is beating his meat
no screaming today is heard from the hole
and the criminals are out on the street
of Justice Supreme there's no end in here
of men's crimes just a beginning
bad jokes and cow pokes,
hippies and farmers,
rapers and stabbers,
robbers and harmers,
together they sit,
killers and charmers
in a pirate's steel dungeon
brim with moist cold
or sweltering hot if late in the day
the remorse of their sins
their hearts do hold
and some even kneel down
to God and pray

Ursus Horribilis Californicus.... 1981

on my back
and in my mind
you still remain,
tho since '22
you've not walked
the forest with me
nor tasted the fruit
of the manzanita
shining crimson
in the dawn,
nor the first ripe
blackberries
of autumn,
juicy and sweet
like your blood
must've been
as it flowed
from that most wicked
wound
which sealed forever
your ancestral tomb

The Making of a Poet Part Two
The Weaklies
1980 - 2017

The Weakly Chronicles started in 1980 while I was in prison with very limited access to the news or happenings in the World. I was forced to condense my reactions to current events and headlines read from a newspaper posted on the wall outside of my cell. Mt. St. Helen's erupted the same day as I did, and that is where I start. I have kept The Weakly Chronicles as my key to sanity in this insane world in which we live. This episode of 36 years will close today as Aleppo is evacuated, Americans are still being held captive in Iran, and we are once again speaking of nuclear capabilities. Personally, I was expecting more progress from my fellow Human Beings.

Mt. St. Helens 1980

THE WEAK THAT WERE.... MAY 1980

While free Americans
are held
captive by Khomeni
St. Helens spews forth
fire and ash
blacks in Florida
erupt in violence
as the Toutle floods
with once-were firs
and the oceans
with refugees drowning
and gasses loosed
by the Russians in
Afghanistan
creep closer to the

lungs of the World
so please don't use
your wood stove today,
the pollution index is critical
and the inverted atmosphere
is trying to choke us
in our own exhausts

Islanders in the South Pacific
have been allowed to return
to their reconstructed
nuclear test site
after thirty-five years in exile;
where in hell will the people
of Pennsylvania go
while we try to forget
where to hide the wastes?
eat it, masticate, swallow it
Mother Earth
but please, oh please
don't spit it out
like you did at the
Love Canal,
or piss it away
in the Colorado, Ohio,
or the mighty
Columbia Rivers
to the cesspool
of the Pacific
the fish aren't that hungry
the birds aren't that thirsty

in an election year
the government has lost
a half-ton of their opium stash
needed to kill the pain no doubt
as bobcats, eagles
and the gainfully employed
all face extinction
the grizzlies are already gone

teary eyed we flush
our pupils
with the acid rain only to cry
again for the songwriter,
musician, professor
of love lost
to the ultimate critic
a crazed by-product
of our deteriorating society

that has prisoners
sleeping on concrete floors
as there are no beds left,
there is no more space
altho we spend billions
exploring it
from a budget
which is managed
by the select handful
appointed by those
barely elected
by only half of half
of the voters...
do the rest not care?

or had they long ago lost hope
and voice
their frothy dissents
over a beer at the local tavern,
or dreamily
o'er a joint at home,
of good grass which
should be grown locally
and soon I guess
for taxation of course
for what else matters?
the money's the crime,
or the lack of it;
the distinction is thin
nearly nil like the virgin timber
left in the forests
and in the memories
of the old loggers
who cut the last back in '54

ten years ago
we brought the war
back with the Warriors
we couldn't win over there
so to make them feel
more at home
we continue the use
of 2-4-5-T in Oregon
it's like we never left
as if our bodies needed
more poisons,
as if our babies needed
no more hope;
and fearing the future,
would-be fathers
have stopped the growth
of their family's tree

but to right the wrongs
the ex-president is suing
the country,
a citizen now, he like everyone,
can sue anybody for anything,
for we are all full of suits
and the ability to
twist and mangle
our words, your words,
my words
to mean not what I said,
you said,
we did not say and,
by God I'll sue you
for that too!

WEAK 2.....1980

Now, with a shudder
of disgust
our planet flaunted
its' faults again today
burying thousands
amidst the rubble in Italy,
and in Algiers
a broken-legged baby
was born to a dying mother
who snipped his cord
while underground
to separate their deaths
by more years
of post-natal agony

WEAK 3....1980

Our skies turn black'
with the mountain's vomit
which settles again
o'er twelve states
and flies round the world
and I, in my cell
that protects society
from me
can only cry in anguish
because I cannot reach out
with my hand
and help right the wrongs
we have done

WEAK 29......1996

Our planet flexed
it's muscles amongst
the weak again
and rumbled down
in Mexico as a reminder
that she is still strong
despite NAFTA
but weaker yet
is the stock market
which tumbles so well
it should enter
an Olympian event for
style with no grace

but leniency does exist
here today in our courts
as our heroes walk free
to pursue
their millionaire sports
despite cavorting
with the devils' own drugs
and showing off
their own
human weaknesses
in this very weak
and feeble moment here
in Archaeology Today

ANOTHER WEAK 1996

Would-be candidates
drop swiftly bye
letting the left handed shaker
gather steam and futilely waste
resources and time
after another campaign
of negativity and promises
that will always be broken

while in the mid-east
the war rages on
and while the number
of volunteers willing to strap
explosives to their chest
have diminished
it is not enough to suit
my mind
nor the minds of the Israelis
next door,
nor Yassir, himself

Uncle Russell died this week,
as did another Burns
with two hundred years
between them
one just short,
and one just past
the century mark
but both walked
with grace and smiles
and lived the life that
no one else could've lived
but them

now today,
another terrorist arrives
in the land of Burns
shunned by twenty years
of misunderstanding
to relay that
misunderstanding
upon sixteen families
of children
gunned down in Scotland
by years of misguided anger
swelled up within
awaiting a final match
for to lite his fuse

which only proves how
vulnerable we are
to the solicitations
of the Great Solicitor,
that he, as the one to which
we must answer
calls for us at any moment
while unsuspecting,
some of us who wish to go
must stand, agape,
in wonder,
in awe while others
are called
before us, again, this time

A Weak in 98..... 1998

More terrorists
attack against the weak
as more unlikely faults
have claimed
a score or more
of unsuspecting,
undeserving
and unguilty

while the seat of terrorism
objects to sanctions
and closes its' doors
to inspecting nations
saying you cannot look
for something
we do not have
but we're sure not going
to let you find it here

and over here
the terrorism continues
at random as
at schools and restaurants,
terrorists flaunt
their disregard
for the citizens,
who take the brunt
of the forces
against the government

that happens to be
spending deficits
on sex these days
that the immorals
don't care about,
the morals
don't understand,
and besides
the dry cleaner
destroyed the evidence,
of who may have been

THE CRUISERS, BONNIE AND CHARLES.....1998

The cruisers took off
in secret flight
a hundred some intent
on the destruction
of a madman's training camp
and a factory of terror
in the dark land
a half world away
threats of more terror
from the dark land
takes second place
to the natural outlaws
of Bonnie and Charles
who deluged Del Rio
and are poised to take
the Carolinas by storm

already dead
are a dozen and more
and nearly dead
is a New York teen
who is paying
for brandishing
a much too lifelike
weapon of terror
in a much too
terrified world
that hides the facts
that over three thousand
have died in China

and fourteen million
homes have vanished
from the fields
but still,
that news pales
next to Bill's escapades

then terror starts anew
today at The Planet
with more dead
and even more injured
as the Madman claims
the innocents
while offshore
the outlaws lurk
with yet another lady
behind her whipping
winds and waters

9/11 THE DAY OF THE WEAK....2001

The world became silent
today to the rumbles
as the two towers
fell down amongst
onlookers both near
and far in disbelief,
anguish and fear

fires, smoke and debris
mingle with politicians and police
who themselves mingle
with dead firefighters
all trying to help
the unhelpable
professing possibilities
in a world
of impossibilities
where anything is possible
especially in a world
of technology
and civilization,
that we seem to forget
is responsible
for the procreation
of man in his
inhuman guise,
with his inhuman mind

and yet we continue
to attempt
to create a human being
from a single cell
but have we found
what or who
that single cell may
become or truly was
since we have already
been and have already
known our past,
whether we really know
it...or not

and whether or not
we return
or whether or not
we are worthy of returning
or simply if the next life
is beyond and beautiful
our journeys
will never be forgotten
our journeys will never
be forsaken

as our hopes stretch
to the days beyond
we cling to pictures
and memories
always in hope, that the singular
thread that binds us is love
in times of hate
when God embraces us all
and in the name of God
this terror strikes
into the heart of all
civilization
when it is not
in the name of God at all
but in the mind and for
the name of the unnamed
that we all know

God no, not he,
though he exercises
those same rights,
those same duties
as the real God must do,
not the other's,
to tend to his own garden of time
which is in need
of some serious weeding

while the Nations weep
to water the ground
and the skies blossom
whilst the redness
of the blood let
whence the parts parted
and were scattered
beneath the rubble
of the fittingly named
Battery Park

which is now hallowed ground,
as much as Auschwitz
and Pearl Harbor
where other men and women
fell prey to madmen
playing God in a flawed role
In the theater of man
on an island stage

THE WEAK OF THE INAUGURATION....2004

Gone is yesterday
and the limits it imposed
for today is a new day
the old party deposed

so when we awaken
tomorrow a new we
we will be
in attitude and strength
resolve we will yield

to lesson the chains of the past
and find the reins of the now
to wet our appetites for that
next leap of faith

THE 7TH WEAK OF THE NEW YEAR

Have the Politicians embarked
on a business career?
to manage the money
of the People, by the People
and for the People
as if they have the experience
to know best over weaks
for all and above all else
as if it were experience
and not the votes
that drove them to the office

they still grapple with facts
that show the other fifty percent
of those who would not vote
did not vote, will not vote
are not as dumb
as they must think
as we breathe the same air
and sun under the same sun
but the water we drink
is a different sort

and crimes are also
a different sort
for those whose investments
take advantage
of the weaks
just another way
to beat them down
whilst they go up
in gains and
down in honesty
unrepentive
just awaiting
the next time the weaks
will need advice
on voting......or not

THANKSGIVING WEAK....2010

Again it is hostages
held against
their will for the will
of their captors
who believe in beliefs
that only succumb
the weakly willed
who then kill
the weak and unwary
to prove their strength
but they are weaker
then even the weaks

CHESSER CAT SMILE... 2010

The Chesser cat smile
seems timely in the
world of Alice
and her wondrous lands
where all is not
as it seems as
Khomeni still holds captives
not much has changed there
except the price of fuel
to keep us warm,
and deliver us to
our government jobs
in order to pay the beast
for its' dietary regimen
of growth with the
sweet dessert of power
and control,
the ultimate authority
o'er the weaks each week
who must live
week to week
whilst the preyer prays

ANOTHER WEAK IN MARCH.....2011

The bomber
has been bombed
that's the bomb
that exploded this week
as across the dark continent
the innocents cry loudly
for their voice to be heard
above the lowly greed
of those that have
ruled the ruled
for oh so many
unruly years

while in Japan the pieces
are being picked up
through and through
and piled high
as the numbers of the dead
raise up to touch the skies
with an angel's hand
and sparingly, hope still flickers
as miracles appear
where darkness once fell

re-uniting generations
of skipping souls
still with life to live and love
to remember those days
and wait
for what they do not know
for when they do not know
for how they do not know
for why they will not know
all the while knowing only
that they remain the weak

TRIPOLI AGAIN...2011

From the shores of Tripoli
we watch, we launch,
we wait and we wonder
simultaneously filling the tank
full of empty promises
of the rhetoric of right
and rights of all beings
but we are NOT all beings
nor ever should we aspire
to forsake that
which makes us us
is to but forsake
being us altogether
and we remain
the weaks

THE WEAK 11... 2011

This weak ended
with the beginning
that pushed
the coast of Japan
far inland,
washing away,
wiping dirty,
burying beneath
the wave everything
held sacred, secret
and sanctimonious
'neath its rubbly
rumblings that quiet
those unmoved
who screamed their last

the world watches,
the world waits
for the arrival
of the remnants hoping
the ripple is small,
the beach stones move
to their new homes
with a gentle surge and nudge
from the Mother
as she rearranges
the jumbled mess of
the remnants
of humanity

The Last Weak of February.... 2011

As the ancient world unravels
from the navel thru the heart
of uncivilized civilization
our hopes and prayers remain
with those of pure heart
and souls that know not
of the freedoms inferred
nor rights inalienable
as their leaders of decades
slaughter them in the streets

they gather above to watch
as the bodies are buried
in mass graves with no names
below the norms of now
and above the coming apocalypse
forced by the last remaining
despots, who strive to control
the uncontrollable
by binding their arms
and shooting them in the head

the same place they have been
kicked repeatedly, until now
as the networks have bundled
informed and empowered
the peoples of the heart
and the souls
of the souls

Two Weaks before Christmas....2012

Where do you start writing
after a tragedy as this?
what are we doing
with our youth?
is work so important
that legacy loses
the hope we hope for,
for as I go you go
and though more
were killed in Syria today
the devil hits home
more immediately
when it is our own children
which makes us
the ultimate hypocrites
for the feeding frenzy
that fuels the fools
that feed upon that frenzy
and are fooled
by the fools' notion
that our children
will not be fooled
but they are fooled
and they are killed

The Annual Weak in Review...2014

It was a great year
for a good dog
not so much for
politicians, cronies and
journalists who lost their heads
on film as social media
watched unashamed
while lies abound
near as deep as the snow
which arrived early in some places
then washed down stream
and across oceans
cleansing the earth
with dirty mud
the mud emerging
in politics and protests
for all the wrong reasons
courtesy of
a sharp tongue
and pressed suit
that riles the young,
killing them one by one

all this time the commander plays
the back nine that is tougher
than ever he says
as his drive fades sharply
to the rough
where the officers had parked
for lunch
served by another
misguided misfit whose ranks
have swelled as the weak watch
from their couches,
easy prey for the fox
and others who tell their stories
for dinner
eaten raw by those
on administrative leave
paid for by those
that work for less
above the laws written
for someone else
not for them
as they rise above it all
conveniently hiding,
losing their records
and stealing the secrets
of the people
a collage of cronies accepting
the frauds
while the people say
what the heck?

we are no longer
openly stupid dolts
just too lazy to not accept
the call of duty
honorable, but the pay is good,
the time off plenty
the issues dauntingly left
unresolved like a budget
that no one can live with
a prison and war
that falls in to the same
fates as the unborns
and the monsters
who keep the courts a courting
making up new reasons
to charge and justify
the law school admission tests
for we need a lawyer
for everything except,
well, there are no exceptions

we are not allowed to talk
with each other without one,
but three are even better
to insure justice is served
like dinner late and cold
like the conscience of killers
who have no conscience
nor reasons for going to
the school or office
not for education
nor work, but to kill
their degree is

terror and murder
as our sons and daughters
come home
from a war far away
in our backyard
that will not be contained
without us so fall back
to the front yard we will

that will that brought us elections
that still do not count
more than half of voters
cause that is all that care
to share the burdens
of life's decisions undecided
that undoubtedly
will remain undecided
in the fifteen to come
cause nothing changes
we are used to that and gladly
we accept our fates
because we are, after all, the weak.

CALIFORNIA DREAMING...2015

A nightmare best describes
what we hear from the scribes
our leader cautions and sides
with the woman beaters,
haters, fanatics
of Muhammed
the Prince of Peace no more
no less Peace
no more Prince
yet armies they gather
and weaks get killed
as time travels on and on

warriors they are not
but murderers of the weaks
they are that no doubt
dozens are getting shot
with no stake in this business
but sense it will not produce
but many dollars it will
for those who believe
this is not something new
but something old,
and not unlearned

they take, they rape, they kill
in the name of the Prince
but in the name of the Prince
it is not Peace anymore
but an excuse
for all out war
the weaks will be the losers
no matter who the winner is
there never is
one that won
for they all fear the weaks
who know not
how to be strong

ORLANDO....2016

Last call was called
to the weaks
and the door of death
opened unopposed
as religion again reared
its' ugliest head
taking the souls
of the good and kind
whisking them away
to the here never after
leaving behind a trail
of blood and tears
questions with no answers
solutions with no problems
parents with no children
and lovers with no loves

misintended politicians revel
and force more
weaks to be weaker
when the burden
is not theirs to carry but
the gargantuan government
cannot carry the load,
no matter the cost
or the consequences
of their slips and fails
and the inadequacies
of the wheels they turn
that they hope run smooth
without a single toe
tred upon
without a single feeling hurt

forgetting all the time
the history lessons
and rewriting
those same lessons
purging them from books
and classes
to make them palatable
and easily digested
while real problems linger
unafraid they prey
upon the weaks
week after week
year after year
in unchanging themes
amid promises by
the elected
and fratalities of
the electorate...
when will the weak
become strong again?

THE WEAK OF OCTOBER....2016

Again in Italy
the Master's works
have painted rubble and death
o'er rolling landscapes
and vines of centuries
that interlaced generations
now separated never to be
whole again with history

aftershocks and foreshocks
with more fores to come after
the people needing to rest
on their cots with eyes open
ears open, and senses tuned
to the shaking and rolling
of their ancient countryside

nothing saved, nothing sacred
not even the basilicas of prayer
that heard the confessions
before and beyond belief
while under the rubble comes
muffled cries growing fainter
and fainter while hope dims

and the inevitable waits
and lingers........

THE WEAK OF THE TIDES.....2016

Meanwhile, as the Tide rolls
New Zealand was rocked
with the false flood
of staunch disappointeds
of yet another election
thousands of miles away

as their time to pack
is cut short by their yearning
to burn and break glass
in protest of protesting
never willing to give peace
the chance
that Lennon wanted

but we are still at war in Iraq
Afghanistan and Syria too
where we watch on the news
ever so slightly their progress
that is over shadowed and
hidden from us,
subbing the fights of politics
with lies exposed,
realities exaggerated
insults flying
as low as drones aloft
while millions flee the terrors
of life with no where to go,
with no hope to get there

like the veterans who return
that must sleep in the streets and
just like in war they dream
sometimes of better times
to come and promises
always the promises
then always the reality

for the reality are the faults
which midnight flaunted
far away causing
the sea to dip and rise
like the weekend battles
and losses
but the Tide rolls on
unbeaten

THE WEAKS AT THE POLLS.... 2016

18 months, and millions, nay billions,
spent to lobby for a position
that pays a fraction of that
to head a government fractured
except in the hearts and minds
for it is the need of ultimate power
that fuels and drives the bus
for the rest of us

only to find the truck stop
diner is out of pie,
there is only cake left
with coffee newly brewed,
threats and expectations
expected anxiously
and served hot with good gravy
o'er a mash of goodly hash

instead it is a bark that we get,
crying foul again
as we must always be right
for we did get an award
for participation, so certainly
we must have won the race
in our minds towards the goal
of what we do not know, nor care,
but the goal is the goal for now
and we participated
after all

so while one team trains for
the next quarter the last team
strains, the voters and await
the next half, not licking
nor caring for, their wounds,
yet breaking glass, marching
towards Chaos, settling in ranks
while Bama rolls on still

THE HAVANA WEAK....2016

Five decades later
Fidel leaves Cuba,
but with typical flare
was stuck in the road,
being stubborn I guess
still flaunting his powers
midst the sweet smell of
the cane that started it all

meanwhile, the pipeline
is halted, for now,
cause no one can make
a decision stick today
they just run away and hide
after the deed is done
but now at least can smoke
a decent Cuban cigar

placating is now a course
in the political university
and a failing grade is
acceptable and the norms
where respect and honor
are no more, only the votes
and endorsements for cash
cause it is still the monies
that rule us,

even though we did not
pay the Native Americans
with anything other than
a bad deal to begin with
now it will be in the court
of the Dealmaker, so we will see,
if honor lies artful and warm,
or coldly in other venues
so bundle up for the storms
coming soon as we wait
and watch the horizon
for another Crazy Horse
to lead and cry foul
leading the strongs and
the weaks together
in protests and victories
that will last forever

heralding, fitting this season,
a new beginning of honor,
cherishing commitments made
long ago, never to forget,
never to modify
as we have our own
Constitution
to suit the suits of powers for
....wait for it.....
the money...of course!

or revenge when the decision
does not meet expectations
based upon bias not facts
which are yet to be found
but still we must cling
to our Constitution or
we start hanging everyone
on a tree to begin with,
but then the suits would be
out of work, and a burden

ALEPPO AND POINTS EAST.....2016

Come out
in the streets...
it is safe....for now
believe us
we will not harm you
nor rain barrel bombs on you
while our guns reduce
the weaks that survived
the weeks of unending
reigns of power
with no powers
no waters
no nothings
but rubble and dust
to which they will
soon become

while a half world away
the news is dwarfed
by politics big
as the prize is contested
as they want
an instant replay
and the challenge flag
is thrown in the face
of the weaks
but that is a penalty too
of the desperation
frustration and defeat
as the weaks were stronger
finally signaling
enough.....is enough
we want to be strong

the whole world wants
to be strong
if it weren't for the weaks
that linger with no hope
that hunger for no food
that thirst for no waters
that love for no reason
those that will die
those that will live
and those
that still hope
so why East Aleppo?
it is only fill already
for a pond not dug
but dry and large enough
to bury the weaks
but the weaks have left
leaving more room
in Aleppo
and Americans
are still in captivity

THE NUCLEAR WEAK ... 2016

Talks again of the BIG bomb
when the weapon of choice
is a truck in a crowd
for lack of vigilance
and polite hesitations
so as not to offend
nor terrorize innocents
women, children and the feeble
are the only ones
they can conquer
as we watch from afar
withdrawing from the world
escaping to warm islands
not to be bothered by those
who stand with us thru time
and space, as that is the quarrel

space, the vastness explored
by legends and hopes
for the ultimate escape route
of the weaks to lands
that may be weaker than they
when they land
just as we all have landed
launched from other
cities and countries
and vetted
that's a new word
that every country knows
and pays dearly for failing
in its' meaning

for there is always a way
around the rules
it can be found in baseball
like the DH rule
or interference
as well as the law
that is written by those
that break the law

this is proving to be a
Helluva weak
the button the button
where is the button?
who has the button?
just kidding...
as there is no button!
but the president
visited Hiroshima
after being in office
for seven years and today
the Japanese visit Pearl Harbor
and I really have to wonder
why they waited so long
maybe our next commander
will visit first
to fully ponder what happens
when you push that button

THE TURKISH WEAK

Another night club and
Dozens more never saw the New Years
come in nor able to taste
the champagne as
only blood flowed
in the glow of sparklers
and the firing of the gun
across the dance floor
as THEY cannot
wage war upon warriors
they wage war only
upon the Weaks
as the Tide keeps rolling
but not for long
as the Tiger creeps

THE PASSING OF SPIRITS

It was shortly after the realization that the life of a songwriter was not in his future that Johnny Half a Horse started another summit attempt on Mt. Hood. That realization had occurred after spending the past 30 days listening to the radio, after which he concluded that all the great songs of country music were taken from the days of his life.

There were, however, always mountains to climb. He was alone, just as he liked to be, except for the Spirit of his Great Grand Father, who accompanied him where ever he went.

Oh, Half a Horse, it is a good time of year when the glacier is still frozen, and yet the buds of spring below bring a vibrance to the sights. The sun warms the earth and the ice remains frozen.

Working his way up the glacier face with his ice ax and crampons digging into the cold, hard slab of ice, he was intent and sweating in the freezing temperatures. This was his world: ice, sun and steepness. In another thirty minutes or so he would walk upon the summit of the mountain, as he had times before. That was his place, his and his Great Grand Father's. On top of the mountain he would take in the view of the world below.

Half a Horse, this has been a good day to climb. We are close, you and I, up here near the clouds and sky. You, who are the son of the son of my son, look at this thing that you have now done. Tell me again what is most important to you: the top of this civilized mountain or the insanity of the uncivilized world below. Touch me Half a Horse, just as you did when you would tickle my feet with the Raven's feather as I napped. Even though I was dying you thought I was merely sleeping. It is a wonderful sleep, Half a Horse, a very wonderful sleep.

A smile appeared on Johnny Half a Horse's face as he, too, remembered that day his Great Grand Father lay dying many years ago. He was a boy of just five years and had picked up a Raven feather to tickle him in mischief. He did not understand dying, or death. Johnny still remembers the smile that came across his Great Grand Father's face just before he went to 'sleep'.

Yes, Half a Horse, to pass in to the lands of our ancestors you must have a smile upon your face as well as peace in your heart. On the day of my journey you gave me the smile I needed to finally pass.

Paper Airplanes & Serial Lovers is a collection of poetry and prose inspired by a lifetime of experiences, some good and some bad.

Part One of this book tells the scope of some of the author's many life experiences including being a young Marine in Vietnam, a wandering biker, rock climber and in prison for Manslaughter. The loves lost along the journey still haunt his mind.

Part Two is inspired by the frailties of the human race and the powers of nature. The hypocrisies' of government are also revealed such as when the State of Arizona felled the famous "Shoe Tree" on US 95 because it was deemed a 'traffic hazard'.

Shoe tree US Hwy 95

The author lives, works and writes on San Juan Island, WA.

CPSIA information can be obtained
at www.ICGtesting.com
Printed in the USA
FSOW02n0231200717
36550FS